I0755919

FINISHING LINE PRESS
www.finishinglinepress.com

A Moth Collection

poems by

Anna Ojascastro Guzon

Finishing Line Press
Georgetown, Kentucky

A Moth Collection

ISBN 979-8-89990-455-4 First Edition

Acknowledgments

"How to Live Large: A Debate" *McSweeney's Internet Tendency*. 2005.

"Her Defense" *Best American Poetry Blog*. 2009.

"We Bitches" *Best American Poetry Blog*. 2009.

"How to Cope with One's Mother-in-law" *Best American Poetry Blog*. 2009.

"Lily Feet" *Bone Bouquet*. 2013.

"The Island" *Anak Sastra*. 2014.

"The Homeland" *Anak Sastra*. 2014.

"Notes on Emerging" *The Boiler Journal*. 2015.

"Lot" *The Boiler Journal*. 2015.

"Homestead" *Dulcet*. 2025.

"Solution" *Dulcet*. 2025.

"The Citizenship" *The Bellingham Review*. 2025.

Publisher: Leah Huete de Maines
Editor: Christen Kincaid
Cover Art: Maria Ojascastro
Author Photo: Jennifer Korman Photography
Cover Design: Elizabeth Maines McCleavy

Order online: www.finishinglinepress.com
also available on amazon.com

Author inquiries and mail orders:
Finishing Line Press
PO Box 1626
Georgetown, Kentucky 40324
USA

Contents

For my family, friends, and mentors

Specimen

It appears as a lollipop that has fallen to the floor and picked up lint and ant legs as it rolled. It is a living larva. Corpulent and white. But it was once a moth, with fuzz on its wings, discerning the possibilities of light bulbs. If winged a second time it will not find itself behind scrapbook wrap again. It will eat the net before it is pinned.

The Citizenship

We were told to ground the rattles of snakes into a powder
and mix it with water to form a solution
that will ease the suffering of childbirth
and prevent the foliage from turning red
and yellow. The pigments rise to the surface if left
unchecked, drawing in every last packet of light
that it can, pocketing the change in case it's needed
for later. Or if a grey heron needs to make a call
at a payphone to say she's running behind.
"A traffic signal is broken. And everyone is waiting," she says.
"What a mess," her husband replies, with a sigh as he peers
through the blinds, at the leaves that swirl and dive
in the wind, like a fleet of paper airplanes crashing.

How to Live Large: A Debate

She said she'd take Ella's voice
The pixie frame of that Broadway dancer
Maybe the anatomy of Heidi Klum
And Frank O'Hara's charisma
She'd be a poet. And live in New York City
She'd be a flirt. She'd be young

I said, "I think I'll sleep around. I'm not afraid of dying young
I'll even take out an ad in the Village Voice
Saying, 'Hey hot town, New Girl in the City
With the flexibility and endurance of a dancer'
But who needs an ad when you have Clinton's charisma
And I can always buy the body of Heidi Klum"

She said, "We shouldn't feed the pressure to clone Heidi Klum
We should inspire girls who, like lambs, are tender and young
Let's start a magazine for women and call it Charisma
which will be like Allure but with an edgier voice!
It's audience will be the corporate, single-mom dancer
Who loves the Rock 'n Roll on which we built this city"

I says, "Fuck that, I'm goin' to Oklahoma City
Movin' in with my best friend, Heidi Klum
I'll work as Tina Turner's back up dancer
Or remake Tambourine Man with Neil Young
I'll attend OU and major in voice
I don't got talent but I sure got charisma"

She said, "You'll start a cult with all that David Koresh charisma
You ought to make a pilgrimage to Vatican City
You should repent. Finally hear the Lord's voice
You can change your name to Sr. Mary Heidi Klum
Commit your life to translating the works of Carl Jung
into Latin as penance for your days as a dancer"

I said, "Look, you be the writer. Translate Tiny Dancer
into rap then sell it to Seventeen or Charisma
I'm eating ice cream for breakfast and drinking wine while it's young

In the world's most romantic city,
Amsterdam, hometown of Heidi Klum
You'll find me singing My Way in an operatic voice"

She said, "Your charisma has moved me, although I'm not young
I'll be a line dancer in Salt Lake City,
If I can't have the voice of Ella or the tits of Heidi Klum"

She Changed Her Name to Judy

She knew it. She wasn't dim
just deprived of sleep: the answer to every ailment
the real-life fountain of youth and city of gold
for which conquistadors risked their reputations
families, and sense of home.
She needed an unmapping of the day
where she could wander freely, while lacking
even a dusk to tell her when
it was time to return for supper. That was the only land
she had, where she could release the pick-ax
in hand, quit chipping away at sulfurous roads
and put an end to that skipping,
that infamous walk, aflame, and the familiar
draw of pyrrhic applause, sparking.

Homestead

Eventually, feelings pass for most. There are a few, though,
who remain enraptured. Imagine. Feeling as if you've
swallowed that fluorescent sunset and kept it
safe behind your sternum, so it never bleeds
beyond the edges of that one afternoon
when you first felt you were a part of every thing
that houses an instinct. The tint of
that memory makes temperatures rise
a half-degree Fahrenheit inside of capillaries.
But you let go of that neon bouquet that flickered
and bloomed arbitrarily, so often that it kept you
up at night. You're a better human than me
for releasing the helium wish. You, instead, plant
your soles into promises, made to your earliest days.

Eulogia

What do you do with all those words you can't say?
The vowels siphon your cells dry, like a raisin
I've heard. Verbs pile up and combust.
Everyone becomes ashes, ashes.
Do you feel a need to feed your syllables?
Or brine them like olives in saltwater, eyeballs
in formaldehyde. A preservation of restraint.
Or may we lay it all out there
like a checkered picnic blanket, a biography
that easily unfolds, like a pleated linen sheet,
or paper fortune-teller that can predict who you'll marry.
Or a one-thousand-year-old bird,
balancing on faith in the stories passed down, leaving
a wake of pauses, an exhaust of throttled words.

Agape

How do they reel in the most agile?
A hardy muscular swordfish
or a shimmering yellowfin? Without fail
the capture is cast back with wounds.
They atrophy or deform before making one tougher
less limber than before. "What doesn't kill
you..." is what one says before seeing
death more than once before.
Before learning to block a hook
a sinker, a-knock-the-wind-out-of-you end to
anything that is familiar. Even sunlight and air
smart. Startle like a bite.
Like venomous lightning-bugs. Again.
Blame her for mistaking the bait
for nourishment.
Will she wise-up to the lore of living happily ever
before she's reeled up,
eyes and mouth agape, unaware?

Elizabeth's Errors

The queen burned all
the old pictures
of auburn on
shoulders. Inborn
pink. No subject
would know a thing
save her I-don't
give-a-damn-air.
Her object was
erasure of
living without
an other, an heir
a mother. Not
even evening
received license
to sense fear.

Peuce

She could create a new fashion trend
be the Marie Antoinette of her district. But
he can decide his own fate.
She's not that woman, that sort of woman, the other
woman, the obscene word that stirs inside
her intestine. For now, she can imagine
a blanket laid beneath the last dark sky.
She could look gorgeous again to someone
who doesn't even want to own her,
who isn't daunted by her thoughts, like a lost dog
that both guards and bites the hand that feeds it.
Sure, she'll ordain herself queen bee of her dominion.
But like an ordinary flea, with a bloodline-filled belly,
she would rather dine on canis major.

A Log in the Eye

I never did dot my I's
with hearts, did you
Ms. Plath, when you were nine
and you believed that fireflies
formed the stars?
I, too, caught
iotas of doubts in a bell
and sat them on the counter
to communicate. You might
have believed that they'd be
better off with someone
other than you.
And who hasn't felt
that singeing flick from the hearth
on the coldest day, on record
in London?

Fluttering

She thinks some relations have a shelf-life.
They go bad from botulinum. Replicating. Bubbling
like underwater talking, between two friends at the pool.
Their sentences are trapped in a pocket
then released into the air and
swallowed by the day's obese heat.
Planets and stars have their shelf life too, she says
as if the universe stamps the underside
of every packet of light, as a reminder to itself
to toss them out with the spoiled milk.
Others say our splinters of consciousness
disintegrate: crystals in a saline sea
past lives fading into a current
conceived when a butterfly fluttered its wings.

How Lonely I Would Be Without AOL

To tell me news about people I don't know:
Who is aiming at random today?
Who is famous? Am I? Did you see me
as I fetched the mail in my husband's robe?
To spend the day in my bathrobe
peeking through the blinds
screening calls on the machine
has always been a dream of mine
an unnerving recurrent dream of mine
which undermines my meditations:
I hope the world finds peace, I repeat
but a glitch occurs in the recorder.
I was once an astute recorder
an able secretary of the class.
I took note of the President's coming
undone before she shaved her head.

Lily Feet

It is not permissible
for her to say she wants

to watch triple X films
in theaters that smell

like the hands of men.
It is not permissible

for her to say she thinks
of the doctor, the patient

the teacher, the student
the waiter and the man

to whom she last confessed.
It is not permissible

to speak of it
even if it's not true.

It is not permissible
for her to say she dreams

of you in your
apartment. She has

run there after a rainstorm
yes, just like in the movies

where the nun is lonely
and the sidewalks are steaming.

BI-ANNUAL MAPLE LEAF HILLS GARAGE SALE: SAT. 7AM-1PM

BIG TICKET ITEMS: Treadmill, Weights Set, Rollerblades, Rancor/ Umbrage

NAME YOUR PRICE: Gently-used Men's Shoes, Vanity, Jealousy/ Envy

FREE: Guilt, A Piece of My Mind, Irreparably Torn Safety-nets, Misc. Housewiferies

SEEKING: Plastic Red-Flyer Wagon, Seasonal Paraphernalia, Light Bulbs

Solution

It's not like I want to live in a movie
in which the improbable happens
to strangers who meet on a bridge
in Paris, in the springtime, and a man
falls hard for his best friend's wife and
everyone is running to their lovers' apartment.
They're running beneath street lamps
that form cones of light in the fog, and I just want to sit
on your carpeted floor and binge reruns of films
from the nineties, where the bride is almost late
for her wedding. I'd like to drink hot coffee
on my front porch in the morning, with you
when there's time to listen to sprinklers turning
and observe the moon dissolving in daylight.

A Crude Map of the Brain

God is on the side.
When all is adequate
one senses Him as
one's position in space.
Love has its locus too
sporadically stirring
then reclining in its groove.
Shame, from an act no
person has seen and words
unearthed, move in
evenly, sinking the land
until a convergence
upon the banks
of a wholly upending grace.

Notes on Emerging

One is thrown into eighteen fathoms, expecting
to steady oneself or graze
a surface underneath yet footing never presents
as an option. For a child, this experience
is, at the least, unraveling. While adults
may marvel: Have I ever known anything?
One feels one's lungs filling with
something other than air
and different from what should be
mundane. This is when one becomes inhuman
some being that does not live
inside a home, with portraits, desk lamps
an upright piano. One becomes an animal.
One that does not own a thing
and has daydreams of death:
a body pinned, an SUV and sweating
shuddering, even an odor emerging
while every warning-siren
in one's vicinity, is resounding.

Inspiration

She spots a fruiting body
gently heaving puffs of air
among the chemical scents
metal limbs and
stirring rods broken again.
It expands within
the plastic dish which in
absently, she ashes.
Patient, controlled, it speaks
as one kneeling in prayer.
When she hears it
there is a soft destruction
a siege
of devils in flight.

How to Survive: A Debate

"This is not about passion,"
she says, while absently biting into chips.
"It's about following God, in whom I trust.
When choosing paths, I consult the family code.
You'll find that faithfulness leads to the fittest
vocation. As simple as aligning two points on a grid."

I say, "I'm giving up everything to live off grid.
Foraging for pineapples is my passion."
"We'll see who wins this match of Survival of the Fittest,"
I say while searching my purse for spare poker chips.
"I'm joining a commune. 'Pineapples for All' is our code.
Only taking our fair share will build a bond of trust."

"Well, better set aside pineapples in a Wells Fargo trust.
Leave the family lawyer names of heirs in a grid.
Just make sure the kiddos are wizzes at code
if you hate real work with a passion.
And I hope your kin are exceedingly fit
so they can live off the land and silicon chips."

"I need a forklift to remove from your shoulder that chip.
I thought you need for nothing when it's God you trust.
Footsteps in the sand but it's Cassandra's shoe that fits.
From the heavens we are shimmering: iphones in a grid
our silent prayers are screenshots of our passion.
The earth: a pale blue dot, in an infinite Morse code."

"Don't call on me when you call a code
blue for your vessels, blocked with embolized chips
and the throughline is lost while you follow your passion
and your commune members, who you no longer trust
are on-line waiting for their piece of the grid
that powers their hybrid in starts and fits."

"Sweetie, if you're wearing it, the slipper fits.
You can't deny your genomic code
nor your high school days on the grid

iron. Off the old block, we're each a mere chip.
Just like one's old man. Trust.
To wear it well is to fulfill the passion."

"I don't trust words spoken in code. A passion
that chips at the grid, which ensnares us
fits the bill we pay for evolution."

Her Defense

Did I pin down
your wrists? Did I
drive this red fruit
down your sweet throat?
Did I eye you
boldly until you blushed?
Was your wholesome heart
made unwholesome by me?
Sweet man, so helpless
beneath my witchy spell.
You let them believe
I was the one
in cahoots with Sin.
My daughters and I
make men our bitches,
is that the story?
Have you tried out
self-control, free-will
you wuss? Have you
tried blaming your God-
damned self for once?
Have you? Have you?

Nature

I'd like a child,
a girl. I would
teach her to be
lady-like, soft-
spoken, happy.
She will have it
easy. She'll have
no weight on her
shoulders or her
waist. Her eyes, wide,
will not blink. Her
feet, small, will tip-
toe. Mind, sharp, will
only speak with
a No. 2
pencil. I will
love my girl more
than anything,
almost. If I
had three more of
the same I'd love
each equally.
I'd shelter girls
from men, the world.
Should one step out,
lose her way, I'd
lead her home and
cast the first stone.

A Novel in Nine

The war breaks.

Resources are scarce.
The oldest boy is sent

down the mountain for food.
The house is empty

when he returns.
His family is split

into different camps.
They do all they can

to reunite.
His mother returns

without his sisters.
His father returns

without his brothers.
The boy never loses

his need to apologize.

Homeland

What she wanted was
to give her child a way

to live better
a shelter, clothes, a guitar

a way to be human
rather than merely fit

a luxury, some say.
She gave her child her

hairline and detached lobes.
She gave her child her smarts

the kind that severs
one into two

divorces flesh from thought.
She gave her child.

For the Heir

Francis was the only one to walk out alive
though she entered the camp with three daughters
all under the age of ten
the youngest, just an infant.
Her thin yet muscular limbs
wrapped around her children.
Her arms and legs weren't enough
defense against a bayonet.

The teacher curled beneath her desk
alone, in her classroom. As bullets
shattered every window, she became
silent, made her heartbeat slow
her breaths, imperceptible
as oxygen molecules entered
her lungs, then her bloodstream
and lined-up, single-file.

It was the smallest of them
who protected their mother's vital organs.
The infant was cradled
against her mother's chest
and abdomen, while the toddler
and the tallest grasped her
body until they became motionless.
Francis collapsed, then remained
still as if lifeless. She prayed

her daughters might still be alive.
Maybe the four of them
could escape, reunite
with the girls' father and brothers.
She waited for maybe hours
until every vibration
of soldiers' boots dispersed
in the monsoon air.

The next door classroom contained the children
of migrants from Vietnam
and Bosnia and Syria
and Afghanistan and the Eastern coast of Africa
and the Western coast of Central America.
The shooter walked past
the seemingly empty room
and entered the class filled with students.

On top of the teacher's desk was a spoon and fork
resting in a bowl, filled with warm
arroz caldo, cooked the night before
for herself and her boys. Her sons
had cleared the kitchen table
as jasmine rice steamed in a pot
with the smallest window from which
the vapor could escape into the air.

The Quiet Award

I was so quiet they put a pin on me
and sat me in the corner of
the classroom, an earnest reward
for being so easy to teach.
I'm not always perfect
but it was a platform

I had to maintain to atone
for my mother storming
away from her town
between the mountains
and the China Sea, to a city
in Kansas, where she treaded

in snow, for the first time
in sandals, the best brand one could
buy from the market in Vigan
a former Spanish colonial hub.
Locals coursed through the network
of stalls where vendors sold products

that were gathered by hand, broken
down into parts and reassembled as
gifts: barongs sewn from pineapple fiber
shoes constructed from caribou
skin and sandals that were never
supposed to step on the sidewalks

of South Grand Boulevard and Chippewa Street,
where perfect white snow is churned with debris
from the asphalt roads and rusted trails
and footpaths through prairie flora
unfurling, wild, as if they could fulfill
a mother's most far-flung dreams.

Models of Humanity

The image of human beings as cancerous cells is an example. What we are is clamorous when uncaged and the converse. The collection that performs for a specific function is a similar instance. The symmetrical, those inhibited by dumb Darwinian drive, is another. The conviction for the crime of individual worth invigorates. The stark white pulp of a human, living to comply, may as well be fed to the crocodiles and scorpions.

Dear Mr. Whitman

It was kind of you to write so unexpectedly when I was among my classmates yet felt closest to the addict whose arm we amputated. He didn't find it necessary to get out of his bed. I had burns on my shoulders from turning throughout the night. I'm no genius, Mr. Whitman. I'm just often alone until your and everyone's aloneness wraps an arm around my waist and I don't mind.

Corresponding

Dear OS909,
Sweet things wrinkle when it's hot and she liked pink as a child. The heel of her shoe did damage she didn't expect to the ball of his cherub cheek. She knows she must have crushed the zygomatic and now she wants to depart. But she doesn't get to yet. Wires spark, the puff of smoke leaves. Something else gets inside.
Yours,
OS134

Dear OS134,
Something else, something else? What about pure empty? A powderless pill, a pulpless plum...Have you seen that agonizing diaphanous stare the slump-backed, lump-fish gaze of mom when she sups on tiny cupfuls of air and sings that mercurial evening song?
With sincerest thoughts,
OS909

Dear OS909,
Listen, something pushed it all aside so I think it could happen again. If something could empty into every pocket, furrow and fissure, wash away the curdled and purple, the sour, the thick and the slush, maybe we could find that enough of her has survived.
Always,
OS134

Dear OS134,
But she won't even let one jabber...*She'll say, Careful, honey, your life of clatter of garnish and dough and handfuls of cherries. Of chatter and squawks on tote-bags and totes, of the beautiful people on the screens of TVs. Don't pretend to understand me.*
I think I see what you mean...Something else, something else inside. But you act as if you haven't seen...the child used a bat to shatter his turtle. Taping its shell won't matter.
Warmest Regards,
OS909

Pablum

I'm a mother now. Does that mean I no longer search for ?
I want to clarify .
I question my right to .

The teacher replied, "Sustenance," when I asked,
"Why implant a feeding tube? She's already dead.
Perhaps, we could let her family know."

"How would you feel," asked the teacher,
"If that patient were your mother?"

What would my mother want if she were ?
What would my patient want if I were ?
What would I want, if I were ?

What would I want, if I weren't ?
What does my mother ?
What does a mother ?

Lot

It's arduous work, getting away
not from it all, but from that big lie
that you didn't foresee, when you
were still acquiring a sense, for concrete
buckling beneath you, beside you and
within the most shaded passes
of your periphery, where edifices
are composed of old-town building blocks
the kind that upcyclers relieve
from their lot over-ridden by packs
of collared, spayed and left behind by those
who had too much to roll into their
bubble wrap. "There's no room," they claimed
of the ins-and-outs of their forty years to life.

Bio II

When under the heat-lamps of nature, life revises. —Charles Darwin

Under the heat-lamps of nature, life revises.
Players make unscripted changes
when one's life prescribes a crisis.

And one carries on in disguises
until one's own makeup is strange.
Under the heat-lamps of nature, life revises,

calling for nothing less than autolysis.
Some make the choice to derange
when life prescribes a crisis.

We grieve the loss of vices
when vanity spars with a virtuous binge
but under the heat-lamps of nature, life revises.

Upheaval has its pluses and minuses.
We've all seen a dream house unhinge
when a life prescribes a crisis.

Charting systems of approach entices
us suckers into the fringe.
Under the heat-lamps of nature, life revises,
when one's life prescribes a crisis.

Harrowing

You grabbed your chance by a hair.
Your chance to die a hero's death
in your yellow, two-seater airplane.

And what a sight it must have been.
Wolves and vultures have eaten your corpse.
But your headstone is on the pampas.

Gold fillings, eyeglasses, compass, all
that was left of your carcass, was buried
with you, in case you need currency

in your next life. But I don't worry
for you. You always got by
with your wit and wile. And that face.

I hope it comes back to you. What a waste,
we used to say, for you to have been a priest.
We know. Such is duty for the youngest son.

Every new start of the hunting season
brings dreams of you alone.
We speak as if you're still here.

The Passion

How simple it seems
the gesture between
two friends or mother
and young. But from
where do the instincts
to osculate come?
All at once, one can
see smell hear touch
and taste. Accepting
such encompassing
inspection takes trust.
Once one chooses
to betray, why not
misuse the kiss?

Automated

Him: *running*
Auto-complete: *soldiers, from*

Him: *ken*
Auto-complete: *Doll, next of*

Him: *reason*
Auto-complete: *Blue Skies, Central Park, driving fast with the windows down*

Him: *why*
Auto-complete: *the neighborhood beach, the fenced in garden, the playground by the lake, the church filled with light, feeling guilty about living such a good life.*
It doesn't seem possible anymore.
Was it ever really there?
Or was it just a Rorschach?
You were utterly thankful everyday. You loved your home, every room, every corner of the yard. It was more beautiful than you ever imagined for yourself.
Others loved that life too.
They traveled the world and decided
on that same piece of eternity
that we weren't good enough to have without breaking. How vacuous is one who is impossible to fill? Or are you crackling, glass poised to shatter?

We Bitches

Even a charming little girl will
print a few well-chosen words
neatly fold it into a star and
disseminate her harm. We know

how to ruin a reputation. We learn
to play it in the schoolyard.
Her name sounds like stink.
His eye-ware is hilarious. We grow-up

to make-up assumptions
that are sounder than children's.
His middle name is unfaithful.
Her marriage is laughable. We die

without ever knowing
what is said in one's obit.
She often kept to herself. The bitch
knew how to choose her words.

I Look Fine in Bi-Focals

I've quickly turned. Like organic fruit, left-over take-out
or wine without its cork. But it may be for the best.
Take Stilton cheese, for example. Only mature palates
can tolerate its brawn. I don't look like pictures
from just two years ago. I'm not post-worthy
as often as before. But that's how I want things
how I want to appear. Someday
I'll need my knees replaced by titanium.
The shine in my eyes will become
cumulus. For now, I'm deadly cirrus. But
I can still see a face in the clouds and a rabbit
standing as if waiting for tea, served by a hatter
who has gone mad from her craft but who cares
if the table is salvaged or the vinegar used to be port.

How to Cope with One's Mother-in-law:

When she looks
through your bills
while she dusts
unasked, then
tells her friends
your money
quandaries, do
not reprove
what she does
out of love.

Love her in
return. Love
the living
daylights out
of the mother.
Love her in
that special
way that she
loves only you.

My Parents Are Dreaming About Hiding From the Japanese Soldiers Again

And I hide in my Honda Pilot when I'm feeling I'm not enough to speak. You ate syrup sandwiches. I ate fried bologna and rice. And I don't bake enough sourdough bread. Or take my kids to church enough or attend pro-choice rallies enough, or shave my legs or not shave legs, or play board games with my children enough. Or empty my well of empathy enough, or participate in self-care enough, or bring my neighbors warm brownies enough, or send holiday cards enough, or respond to emails fast enough, or brush my dog's fur enough or commit poems to memory enough, practice chromatic scales enough, or compose Italian operettas enough. Or keep myself calm or carry Narcan enough or stop to smell the poppies enough or thank my lucky stars enough or pray to guardian angels enough. I don't place plums in the icebox enough. Or give myself enough credit enough. Or earn enough. Or save enough or donate enough or give in enough or give up enough. I don't enough enough. Enough enough enough enough. I do not Gertrude Stein enough. I do not Dr. Seuss enough. I am not lady-like nor do I walk on my tip-toes enough or put two nickels in my tiny skirt pockets enough. My voice isn't high enough or serious enough or stoic enough or loud enough, or captivating enough. I do not become a hysterical woman enough or place myself on a pedestal enough, or assert myself, or insert myself enough. I don't consent enough, resign enough, or shout enough's enough enough. I don't enough. I enough. Don't enough. I. Don't.

Stealing Beauty

Sometimes one closes in
on that which is symmetric,
perhaps, it glows or maybe
it's what one once had.
We just want to be near
the real, feel what makes us
more than mammals,
peacocks, toads.
What prompts a mother
to never want to cease
staring at the face
of her young? Is it the same
thing that keeps us
reeling and unreeling again?

The Fittest

We're all just trying to survive.
Handed instincts at conception.
Learned our habits as children.
We are animals with books.

We're all just trying to create.
Dance, act, write, discuss.
A being's purpose is to produce.
We're all just trying to conceive.

We're all just trying to reproduce.
One can't always blame one's mom.
They fuck you up, say some.
Art is a mirror, say others.

We're animals with music,
the ability to produce art,
to preserve, to distort
the habits learned as children.

We all have something to admit.
We've turned away from wrecks.
Fit disasters in straight-jackets.
We're all just trying to self-preserve.

We are animals with bibles,
yet we turn away from wrecks.
We all have something to confess:
our instincts bestowed at conception.

Steeling

Herbivorous animals avoid it
because of its bitter taste.
The Missouri Ironweed is known
for its tough stem, its flower-head
the color of oxidized steel, although
the petals start out as a vibrant
plum or magenta hue, which
attracts late summer moths.
Remaining robust in abandoned
pastures, persistent through brutal
winters, dormant memories are stored
as blueprints for the spring.
Its progeny push against decay, born
recollecting mettle.

A Condition of Pain Related to Yearning for Home

Your enduring attempts
to draw close
as if bracing
oneself from the cold
is to a warmth, which has left.

You do belong to a mother, but
your constant rooting receives
air, the smell of sterile sheets.

Nestling fatigues your muscles
which give out to what you know
is already gone, for good.

Cubs

She thought she'd never
jack another in the face, the most
sensory place in the human
anatomy. What brutality
she'd need to dig up
from her gut
in order to stick it
to thin-skinned lips
or a slender bridge.
But only a glimpse
was required of her deep
within. It was an easy decision
when harm was within
arm's reach of her son.

A Butterfly's Invitation

Why not climb inside the tiny
carrier of change?
You can see it for yourself
the ephemeral address
within which a complete landscape
lies, with highways, side-
roads and oceans of wheat or corn.
Or maybe a metropolis
encapsulated
a grid of lights and the pieces
necessary
for the series of reactions
to occur. Then a wreck
kills everything you were.

Refracting

There is nothing that I am
more acutely aware of
than you. The water in your

eyes, the movement of your
brow when you are
overcome by a rhyme or

the refraction of light
on your chair. You are taller
than the counter now. You

used investigate in
a sentence. You still don't
comprehend the word

kill. How you
purse your lips. How you
hold your pencil. How

the presence of a moth is
worth announcement to
the neighbors. I am more

aware of you than
the surface of my skin. You
are the hairs that stand on end

when I am seated
and I am hearing
what I did not know.

Anna Ojascastro Guzon is a writer, mother, teacher, former physician, and co-founder of YourWords STL, a nonprofit organization that uses creative writing workshops to amplify the voices of marginalized youth. She received an MD from the University of Missouri—Kansas City School of Medicine and an MFA from The New School Graduate Writing Program. She has worked as an executive director, programming director, teacher, and editor of thirteen volumes of student anthologies, during her time with YourWords STL. She has received fellowships from UMKC, The New School, and the Education Equity Center, as well as a National Endowment of the Arts Grant for her work with YWSTL. She also teaches for Washington University in St. Louis. Ojascastro Guzon is a second generation Filipino American and the youngest of seven children. She lives with her husband, two children, and dog in St. Louis, Missouri.

www.ingramcontent.com/pod-product-compliance
Lightning Source LLC
La Vergne TN
LVHW090537110826
845146LV00003B/1147

* 9 7 9 8 8 9 9 9 0 4 5 5 4 *